Enter Me
Vol. II

A.E. Allen

PublishAmerica
Baltimore

© 2010 by A.E. Allen.
All rights reserved. No part of this book may be reproduced, stored in a retrieval system or transmitted in any form or by any means without the prior written permission of the publishers, except by a reviewer who may quote brief passages in a review to be printed in a newspaper, magazine or journal.

First printing

PublishAmerica has allowed this work to remain exactly as the author intended, verbatim, without editorial input.

Hardcover 978-1-4512-8394-5
Softcover 978-1-4512-8395-2
PUBLISHED BY PUBLISHAMERICA, LLLP
www.publishamerica.com
Baltimore

Printed in the United States of America

Introduction

Have you ever wished someone could just have a glimpse of what you have seen? Have you ever desired that someone could just take a few steps in your shoes?

Well, that is the aim of Enter Me Volume II. Often times we are on the outside looking in on another person's life. You may never feel what someone else does as we handle similar situations differently. However the key is gaining understanding of what may have shaped, molded, hurt, or even provided joy and peace to that individual.

I have opened my door and the light is on. Will you come inside? Come in and Enter Me.

Acknowledgements

Always first and foremost I thank God. Through his son Jesus Christ, I am more than blessed.

There are so many people to thank who have impacted my life. Please do not hold it against me if you do not read your name. Continue to pray for me as I will and do for you.

I have to acknowledge and thank my Uncle John Allen Jr. (who is probably surprised!) He introduced me to poetry at the age of eight. He supplied books that contained: Langston Hughes, Robert Frost, Baldwin, and others. For some reason they clicked with me! Again, I thank you.

In just about every life there is someone or a need for someone to be real with you. Frances Goss is that someone to me. We have known each other for almost three decades. Through our ups and downs, I can say you are True. I thank you for your encouragement, support, prayers, and everything else (smile) I love you.

To Ms. Sarella Johnson, she provided the first platform which allowed me to share my poetry. She featured me three times with Poetry on the River.

Sherleta Watkins who always kept stating, "What are you going to do? These poems need to be in a book!" Well, here they are. (smile)

To my former Pastor Reverend Queen E. Harris, Alfadia (Faye) Harris, and the Holy Prayerway family. The International Society of Poets held a contest in Las Vegas, Nevada. I was unable to afford the trip. They all became galvanized including my family (The Allen Family) and sowed into me along with their prayers. I will always love each and every one of you.

My great uncle Burnel Shannon. He told and showed many times over the years that as long as I was doing something positive he would be supportive. Uncle, from the bottom of my heart I thank you.

I have to thank Mona Ladziak this fabulous woman always has been there and is an awesome friend and person. Her only request was that she remained anonymous…Sorry.

I also thank Mrs. Yodit Johnson. Yodit is a facilitator and enjoys getting things done. Yodit you are a great blessing.

To the International Society of Poets and fellow poets, after competing and attending your various workshops I gained so much confidence. Such awesome people and great talent may God bless you.

Dedication

I dedicate this book to my children Antonio Jr. (TJ). A handsome son who is maturing into quite the young man, I am very proud of you. Also my daughter Arryn (Tot) who has so much potential and talent, please explore it and use all of what God has given you.

To my grandchildren Antonio III (Al) and Alana (Princess) I love you both so much.

Pastor Reverend Jimmy Townsend (Bishop Frank N. Candor), man I thank you for all of your support, even when you were almost the only one. (smile) You are more than a brother. God bless you.

I also dedicate this book to all of you who have dreams. Please allow me to encourage you to keep dreaming and pursue all of your endeavors. God has given you the dreams now act upon them. Never give up, never become discouraged.

Last but certainly not least, Bishop Stephen Bennett Sr. and Co-Pastor Valerie Bennett thank you for your teachings, prayers, and covering. Also the House of Prayer and Praise family let us continue in Brotherly Love.

Table of Contents

Chapter One: Between You and Me 11
Real Love* 13
Forbidden Love 14
Still 15
What is this 16
Complexities 17
Erratic* 18
Too 19
Apples and Oranges* 20
Our Time 21
Two Ships 22
Every Time 23
I Love You 24
Blinded* 26
No One Like You 27
And Goodbye 28
Keep Moving* 29
Untitled IV 30
Rainbows* 32
Ocean You* 33

Chapter Two: Between Us 35
Everyday People* 37
Enter Me* 39
Back in tha Day* 41
Lies and Truth 43
Faith and Trust 45
Old Man* 46
About Life 48
New Life 49

Vacancy 50
Universal Prayer 51
Promised Land 52
Untitled XII 53
God Bless America 54
 Freedom* 56

Chapter Three: Just Me 59
Beat Down 61
Letting Go* 62
In memory of Alphonso Turner 62
Who Will Cry 63
After Thought* 64
Conflicted 65
 Devil Talk* 67
Somebody* 69

Chapter Four: Between God and I 71
By the River* 73
A day in the life 75
Why 77
Confession 78
Untitled XIII* 80
Untitled XV* 82
Countless Blessings* 83
You Saved Me 84
Untitled XX 86
I am God* 87

Bonus Poem: A Letter of Communication* 89

* *Denotes author's pick*

Chapter One:
Between You and Me

This chapter depicts life between man and woman and/or husbands and wives. Relationships that are new, seasoned, ending, or what turned out to be just relations. I am not stating that I have experienced all of these things but take a look and see what you can relate too.

Real Love*

Incense, candles, and we will bypass the wine.
You and I need to be sober, the connection I seek
with you is spiritual from heaven, not a glass full of
altering liquid that will negatively
influence your mind and invite unclean spirits.
We can let that song run around, but keep the volume
low these words I speak I desire them
to surpass your hearing and get to a place
that you can feel them, a place deep down within your soul

The truth I speak, this love I convey is meant to soothe
every part of you that is hurting, mend what has
been broken, and strengthen every place that is weak.

I hold your hand symbolically, it is your heart you can
place there. The longing I have done for this moment
is priceless

The tear that slowly trickles down your cheek, I pray
that it means you feel me. Do not be afraid to embrace
this love. Let this love rebuild, renew, and once again
allow you to trust.

Waiting…I have done and will do
Loving you…I always have and will continue.

Until roses are no longer red
and the sky no longer blue
Until you understand that I love you

AeA 11/21/07

Forbidden Love

When I look at you
there appears pure beauty
this woman, not a girl but
this presence of everything
I have longed for

When I look at you
Its your eyes, they are so inviting
I become hypnotized. Your smile
so warm that it relaxes me
even the way you walk, so so seductive
like you are calling my name

When I look at you, I dream
something unexplainable happens to me
I feel like dancing, shouting and singing
Then I remember you do not belong to me

When I look at you, I cannot help but
be dumbfounded and yet amazed
that he cannot see
I can't help that sometimes I imagine
myself in his shoes

All these feelings and thoughts
I must keep hidden, because
they are sinful and forbidden
even so…I wish I was he

AeA 12/29/06

Still

One, two, three, maybe even four times
We have tried to be together
Something so right always went wrong

Though apart our love intact
and ever strong
Out of reach but never out of touch

Still envisioning no one
else but you
Still thirsting for the understanding
Still smiling when I think of you

Every day that passes
there are questions I ask within myself

Years have gone by so
I still ask my heart why are you there
and I am here

Time keeps moving but in your love
I am apprehended

Still caring for and about you
Still desiring your touch
Still fighting the impulse to rush to you

I love you…Still

AeA 2/11/07

What is this

This is the first time our eyes have met
yet there seems to be an indescribable connect
I have never felt your touch or embrace
but somehow I feel you and it makes
my heart race

Between us there have been no
words spoken but I hear you and I
know your voice

Now with my eyes closed continuously I
see your face. That moment, that encounter
I cannot let it go

You have become my souls desire
The only course is to quench this thirst
To bring closure and to understand why
I am feeling this way

So the next time our eyes meet
In spite of my lack of confidence
I will follow my heart, take the
first step to find out what is this

                                        AeA 3/9/09

Complexities

A merry go round that will not stop
A roller coaster ride that never ends
The same thing over and over again

Never enough air so difficult to breath
stress, pain, and misery
It feels as though I am drowning and
there is no help, no hero to save me
only someone constantly depressing rewind
and standing still is time

What is happy if you have never known
Is it too late for change
when you feel damned and alone

Too tired to sleep and this has been going
on for far too long
Something that never should have began
now has to end

A vow that was voluntarily taken
now has to be forsaken
Go against God and what I believe
or stay and continue to die inside

What is wrong…What is right
Who decides

AeA

Erratic*

Illogical, irrational the directions
followed so emotional

Over here, then over there
Up is down and down becomes up
Out is in and then you are no where
to be found

You dismiss the thought of stability
What about you and me?

You love me and I love you
but in love I cannot be
With an unstable foundation
there is always instability

You want to do this then that
Where are we going and
where are we at
We cannot build here, too much
uncertainty so I ask again
What about you, what about me?

Roll out with the tide like drifters
lost at sea

AeA 9/09

Too

Too much done that has caused deep sorrow
Too many harsh words spoken that shaded tomorrow
Too many pieces shattered that remain broken
Too many I love yous offered as tokens
Too much unintentional and deliberate pain
Too many tears have flowed that have cast shadows
and brought rain

Too much distrust and too many accusations
Too many sleepless nights filled with frustration
Too late to make up for what is not there
Too late to pretend that you care
Too unstable of a foundation

Where does that leave us…Too slow don't rush

The sad thing is I still
did not want us to end
but without love we cannot even be two friends

AeA 10/24/06

Apples and Oranges*

You bring to me oranges everyday
I greet you and say thank you always
They smell so sweet so vibrant, full of color
You continue to make the effort
without missing a beat

Until I advise that it is apples I need
You smile and say alright and continue
to provide oranges

Again I request apples for I have a need
My request falls upon deaf ears
so again I plead, and again you do not heed

Pondering the sacrifice you make to gather
and the effort in bringing, to remain silent
and just accept it
or do I make yet another attempt to have
my needs met, or maybe your next
offering just simply reject

Is love looming anywhere in this relationship
Why do I need apples…you never ask
Why do you still bring oranges…I do not
want to offend you

How to love, is it like apples and oranges

AeA 12/29/06

Our Time

Tick tock, tick tock
Time keeps on moving
did you ever stop to think
if we were gaining or losing

The clock doesn't operate in
reverse, how much time do we have
any space for a second chance
or time to rehearse

Like sand in an hour glass
out grown and out dated
how much longer will we last

We can fast forward to the age of digital
but that calls for change
from traditional and habitual

Do you see what I see
time cannot be turned back
clearly you need to know
and understand where we are at

Time will move on it cannot
be stopped or even halted
Between arguing, backbiting,
and fighting everyone is salted
May I suggest before the next move
we carefully calculate and not guess

A time out for reflection or end up
out of time and enter lamentation

AeA 7/15/08

Two Ships

Like two ships we continuously pass each other by
most of the time we do not exchange glances
It is because the growing sentiment is we
are just about out of chances

If we were a book we would each have
our own chapter
Needing that much space how could
it read happily ever after

With that much distance we would never connect
Is that best seemingly because of the lost respect

Communication is essential, vital, some say the key
I keep wondering and asking why can't I
talk but to only me
Mirror mirror on the wall, I beckon and call
No answers, no response, but only my heart in freefall

Two ships…No romance, moonlight, or dance
Just another failed relationship…Sunken
no hope or chance

AeA 3/25/08

Every Time

Every time I attempt to write the letter
My hands begin to tremble

Every time I begin to form the words to say
less than whispers depart these lips

Every time I turn to walk away
something brings me back

Every time I try to forget
something reminds me

Every time I try to escape
something grips me
I can't sleep because my thoughts
are of you like a dark déjà vu

Every time I feel like I am making
progress, I find myself standing still

Every time

AeA 8/26/08

I Love You

Did I hear you say that you love me?
Are you sure that you are saying those words to me

Love is not a trip, excursion, diversion, or a vacation.
This will be a journey between you and I
Love goes beyond a night or a day
love is everlasting

Are you sure you love me?

Maybe you just wanted to take a chance, perhaps
it was only for a passionate dance
like the salsa or tango.
For that I cannot be your partner
do not take my hand instead, let it go

It took some time for me to grasp the obvious
that was so plain and simple
my body is a temple
From deep dark depths I was allowed to return and rise
for just one night I cannot compromise

Are you sure you want to be involved? Or after some
deliberation you have become hesitant
My number and name you will not text or call

I believe before we touch, you should feel me
Before a kiss is shared there should be visions of stars
that fill your heart and head and dreams of what heaven
must be like in each others arms

From our conversations, you should know me
If you do not, then how could you love me

Maybe you need some time to think about what love is
Because I have heard people say the word loosely and
I have seen people state the word falsely

Take some time to reflect and allow your
mind to rewind
I am talking about a covenant
that is based on truth and loyalty So…Do you love me

                                                      AeA 6/30/08

Blinded*

I have been fortunate to see
many of lifes splendid things
finest gems, diamonds, and priceless rings

I have seen all types of moons, stars, and
planets never once taking
what I beheld for granted

What these eyes have not seen is the return
of our love, the enchantment

I have seen sunrises and sunsets
from mountains and even a sandy white beach
I have not seen how to reach you my love

A rare sight I witnessed, a double rainbow
arcing high across the silvery sky
breathtaking and simply magnificent
I thought you would see me
I thought you would see us

I could see us in our golden age
sitting on the front porch
lemonade and a tree providing perfect shade
our grandchildren would stop by now and then
we would still be so in love holding hands

I could see loving you beyond this world
and into the next even throughout eternity

I never once saw that you did not love me

AeA 12/22/08

No One Like You

I have been north, east, west, and south
In all of my searching
I am left without a doubt

There is no one like you

Even the least amount of time away from you
leaves this man with childish anticipation
anxiously waiting for an end to our separation

Whether we are speaking in casual conversation,
holding hands in silence, perhaps an escalation
into intimate relations
Our time to me is so valuable and well spent
each moment is precious
My mind is blown and head always spinning
I find myself breathless

Every amount of my love that is measurable
I pour out seeking only more to give
because of you the essence of life far exceeds
pleasurable
Always wishing greater I could do, say,
or provide
Just thinking of you I smile and come alive

The Lord has truly blessed me
I do not have one single complaint
only to suggest that I could love you
beyond eternity
There is no one like you

AeA 7/28/08

And Goodbye

You look at me and I look at you
No words are spoken
You turn away pieces of me begin
to fall away
I stand alone shattered, my heart broken

Over and over in my mind I search for
answers I tire from wondering why
I know there is nothing left but goodbye

So much pain like a cold slow rain…
Will it never end
We were not lovers, we were not even friends
Just emotions and entangled bodies that were woven
mistakenly thought that we were loving
Still, I already miss you
After three years now it is time for someone new
Maybe thats what I will tell myself
perhaps it will help after I realize
for me there is no one else

I turn one last time to see you walk away
and disappear from behind
I inhale and sigh, then softly say
and goodbye

AeA 6/30/08

Keep Moving*

Some people go up, down, in and out, round and round
we keep moving

Take look on our street Dick and Jane are at it again.
After struggling to stay on the same page
twenty years are tossed down the drain, and they
agree its time to go separate ways.
Is this the beginning of strange days?

Over on the next block Bob and Sue, May and Scott
ten years and the other fifteen. Saying what was is now not
and what once was hot has grown old and cold.
You look at me and I you, I still see one not two.

We want relationships to be like flowers
a virtual bed of roses, but sometimes we rub noses.
We have a home not a house. At times I'll take the basement
Just to provide a little peace, sometimes distance, but not an out.

The plan is still forever. With the Lord as our head
we are tougher than leather. Standing through storms
avoiding what seems to be the norm
We remain stable and calm…Moving on

While others go up, down, in and out, round and round
we keep moving

AeA 4/25/06

Untitled IV

As I held your hand I felt the
pulse of your heart beating

Then I observed the look
that was in your eyes
No words needed to be spoken
for what you were saying
No sound needed to be heard

I will hold your heart in my hand
like a mother and a new born child
I love you more than mere words can
ever express
Although I may not say it often or enough
You are my baby, my lover, my lady,
and now my wife

Just as you have given me your heart
I exchange and give you the same

I feel as though we are intertwined
by spirit and soul

So very difficult to stay composed when
you want to lose control
Just know that I love you more than you
will ever know
By my actions each every day I will show
therefore you will never wonder

My jewel, my star I treasure you

brilliantly you stand against and beyond
any other

So proudly do I exclaim what the Lord
has done sending you my way
You are brighter than the sunniest day

Place your head upon my chest
now close your eyes and relax
you have found rest

           AeA 6/30/04

Rainbows*

We see the rainbows
arching across the sky
extending themselves appearing
as if no clear beginning or end

So beautiful, so vivid putting
on such a grand display
but you cannot touch, reach,
or feel them and they
do not last for long

They could be our symbol and our love song

AeA 3/19/09

Ocean You*

When I think of you
A vision of an ocean I do see
So deep you are filled with
such great mysteries

Somehow I never feel overwhelmed
nor as if I am drowning

What often appears on the surface may
not begin to describe what lies beneath
Still you are so inviting, I just
want to dive right in

Covering and drenching me is your love
No matter how much there is I cannot
get enough

Everything looks good on you…
The moon, sun, and stars they agree too

Sometimes I set sail and just let
the currents guide
Fully confident I just ride
Sometimes an anchor is needed
I have to catch my breath
you move me while soul rests
Never ending your love seems
the view changes, but the flow does not stop
Like an ocean…Like you

AeA 11/2/02

Chapter Two:
Between Us

These poems offer a look into Mans relationship with man. I pose the questions and thoughts; Do we still care for and about one another? What about placing ourselves in the shoes of others, to gain a better perspective. This could lead to a much clearer and deeper understanding. Well read on and decide....Selfish or Selfless.

Everyday People*

When you walk or drive pass someone
when you hear about people in the news
do you ever wonder who they are,
ever ponder or ask what is their story

Someone is going through a loss
someone is contemplating ending it all
they no longer want to feel burdened,
the pressure, or pay the cost

Someone is going through emotional strain
while someone else is facing mental fatigue
someone finances have been drained
yet someone says life has lost its intrigue
because they have become sick, fragile, and weak

Just everyday people…
We sometimes stare, and engage in unflattering
conversations, maybe just ignoring them
like they are not there

For someone divorce has taken a grave toll
they continuously wonder how can they go on
Someone has no home, no job
they feel as though they have been robbed

People who seemingly have no names
Who we may not recognize their faces
people who do not have wide or wild acclaim
people who feel forgotten and estranged

Someone who has made mistakes
looking for a new start
society constantly places them in the background
and upon their necks a neon sign
stating don't come around

To their faces is the absence of nobility
to their names no national recognition
to their plight no kindly affection or attention
We say its their fault they themselves are to blame

Someone, somebody, somewhere on a daily basis
they are going through, they are catching it
When was the last time we prayed for the nameless,
the faceless, or even the hopeless
Do we forget that they exist

Those people, these people
They are you, they are me
and we are everyday people

AeA 6/19/08

Enter Me*

There I was in a time when I thought I was living
when I was barely existing
after years of poor decisions and being ridiculed
From deep depths, Jesus lifted me

He saved me from myself and certain destruction
as he began new construction
He did what the doctor could not do
because he healed me

My mind, body, and soul are restored
I am now whole

He did what the judge could not do
because I am now free
He renewed a right spirit within
now only Jesus apprehends me

I am not the same
I am able to look in the mirror
no longer pointing fingers of blame
that included guilt and shame
Problems that once consumed me
I allow no longer because I have
peace through the word of God that gives me the victory

Come one, come all
you are cordially invited to
have your mind, body, and soul
lifted and united
The God I serve can do that for you

just as he did for me
allow him the chance and the opportunity

Tell Jesus…Come on, and enter me

AeA 7/15/08

Back in tha Day*

I was thinking back to a few yesterdays
The old neighborhood and the summer days

The nicknames the kids had like Jabbo,
Whiterock, and Moon
those days passed much too soon

Water being released from the hydrant
everybody getting wet and the kids so excited

We ripped and ran all day
at least til the streetlights came on anyway
You betta not let momma
have to raise her voice, a sore bottom and
at least a week before you got the next play

I remember gathering on the front porch
shucking corn and snapping beans
Taking a break to eat tomatoes
while grandma cleaned the greens

The milk, watermelon, and ice cream man
all made their rounds
I miss the music and their melodic sounds

The watermelon man on the loud speaker
Yelling how sweet and juicy, just to tease ya

We had elders on our block
they did not mind keeping watch

Back in the day we seemed a little closer
now within families, no one knows ya

To all those whose eyes are now closed
That resided on Parker street
I love you and I miss you! Most of all
thank you for being a part of me

Those who have moved on and have relocated
they can relate to the things I say
Just some nostalgia for back in tha day

                                                                         AeA 7/15/08

Lies and Truth

The truth grows and lies spread
Lies are meant to cover, hide, and deceive
Truth is like a beacon hanging on a giant
redwood tree
When you are ready to open your eyes to see
What the truth does is make one free

Lies hurt, kill, and destroy
As they unleash yet another diabolical ploy
Whats the good, whats the use
lies offer misuse, neglect, and abuse

You choose, do what you do

If it is a lie, what is did is never done
without more lies it will unravel and
become undone
If it's the truth sacrifices may have
to be made for it to come through
each have impact, effect, and imprints that
are everlasting

Seriously thinking, it's a no brainer
but for some they are still asking and pondering

You are fighting a battle that you cannot win
for years you have tried it your way
take a look right now this day
How do you expect this to end, or did you

look at the quick fix, even the hustle

and whats hot. My sisters and brothers
I encourage you to seek Jesus the solid rock

No need for an alibi when you choose truth
but you have to provide proof when you lie

AeA 7/27/08

Faith and Trust

I feel the water rising above my knees
nervous and anxious maybe I should flee

Saw the fire and felt the flames
we point fingers and then begin to drop names

That thing we should hold on to most
we give up hope and seemingly start to choke
In God we trust, they say
but I'm thinking am I going to live
to see another day

Overhead bombs fly and burst
people panic and scatter
who can be optimistic
I'm thinking the worst

Someone stated its time to take a stance
most difficult with nervous feet that dance

Will you stick around for the outcome
or like most, will you turn and run
A remnant is all that God requires for his plan
You and I must decide will we stand

AeA 6/5/08

Old Man*

The old man rocked back and forth
in his chair that sat in front of the town store
He was beyond the age of four score
but still when he was not seated in his chair
he had a broom in hand
and words of wisdom in his mouth

He often stated I have been
up and down many roads, ain't
too much my eyes have not seen
I could not have made it
this far without the Lord

Some folk listened, some did not
many said it was old fashioned and outdated
The old man did not raise his voice or argue
He always remained calm and understated

A group of adolescents asked him
why are you always here at the store
The old man sat down and began
to rock once more

He then replied, this is where I want to be
Nobody but my employees, customers, and me
People don't now I own this store and lots more
No education, no family, only one or two friends
If it had not been for the Lord on my side…

Thats what I tell you boys
Nothing like getting to know Jesus

He was at my beginning, he'll be there to the end

Now you know my story and why I give God all the glory

AeA 6/26/04

About Life

What is young becomes aged then old
what is old must fade then die
We shed tears for some then for
others an outcry
No matter how long or short the life
sometimes the question is still why
For me this is the course of life
every day is made special for
everyone of us

This day decide is it God in whom you trust
If I have learned to live
then do not cry or ask the Lord why but
rejoice because Jesus is my choice

If I only existed then shall there be sorrow
For no more grace exists, not another tomorrow
Grieve because my soul will not find rest
Weep because I did not follow God, him
who knows best

Today while it is light, right now
while there is life
This moment will you learn to live
Will you take advantage of the gift
or be neglectful and only exist
Perhaps have your name not written
on eternal lifes list

AeA 8/29/05

New Life

Like a monsoon that would never end
wide spread damage, flooding, and drowning
took place within

Like a tidal wave you have washed it all away
Things have changed and now I have a new name

I did not know what to expect when you began to knock
from this day and forever grateful is an understatement
If only I had known not only could I fly, but possess
the ability to soar
Simply because loneliness, depression, and fear
reside here no more

Finally realizing I am not rejected
but peculiar and carefully selected to be a joint heir in
his priesthood. He is always working things out for my good
I thank the Lord for grace and mercy. They provided
the time for things to become better understood

Often people ask me the question, if roses can blossom
or even bloom through asphalt and concrete. My response
is always with enthusiasm and a resounding yes!
Look at me, relax for a moment and allow me to share with
you my testimony

AeA 6/19/08

Vacancy

Advice is free please listen carefully
Wisdom and knowledge are the key
but it comes with a price, listen attentively

Observation and repetition can take
you to the next level called higher

No complaining about mundane and boredom
its time to catch fire

Snares and pitfalls await to consume those
who become overly anxious and leave too soon
Dead ends and road blocks never cease
for those who often talk too much
then rush only to bump their head and fall
to their knees

A guiding light is present and will be left
on for now, but because of human nature
there will always be a vacancy

AeA 6/21/08

Universal Prayer

Sometimes as I gaze into the sky especially at night
I often wonder and give thought to conditions and plight

the world is larger than all the you's and I's
and if we prayed together it would be
a step that would enrich all of our lives

I pray also for all the children everywhere who
experience exploitation, misuse, and abuse
I pray for hatred and bigotry to cease
I pray for the end of famines and disease
I pray for the world to study war no more
and only remember to practice peace

As I continue in prayer to God, my eyes often
begin to fill with tears
I desperately pray for the answers in
a soon tomorrow and not many years

AeA 12/01/08

Promised Land

They see you, me, and u.s.
We are the epitome of what can be
Tearing down the walls
we have established love, peace, and diversity

No more black, white, brown, yellow
just peace, harmony, and all is calm
so smooth and very mellow

Absent are red states and blue states
right or left, conservative and liberal
Just people joined together not afraid
of acknowledging common ground and mistakes

Love is the key and peace is the standard
It required hands together, shoulders to lean on
hearts to forgive and embracing one another
Looking pass all and becoming sisters and brothers

We can get there from here if the foundation
is Christ…So tell me what is the color of love

Shaking the foundations the rich will assist the poor
we will no longer fear
It is the model that Christ wanted us to pursue
Mirror mirror on the wall, its time to put away
childish thinking, talking, and things

Its up to me…Its up to you

AeA 3/26/09

Untitled XII

An eye for an eye, a tooth for a tooth
someone is going to be blind, someone
is going to need dentures. What does
that say for mankind

They say you do not know about the atrocities,
hurt, or heartache that they have caused
You do not know about the mental, physical,
and emotional pain they have inflicted
So we choose hangings, firing squads, the
electric chair, and lethal injections
We may grant a last meal while we make preparations

Does anyone know the power of forgiveness
how it would spiritually and financially
cost so much less
Does anyone regain a loved one
After an execution or revenge
Is there any real gratification
Have you ever experienced having a
one time foe become a friend
Christ is the Author and Finisher
only he was able to pay the price for all sin

AeA 12/29/06

God Bless America

How can two walk together unless they be agreed
simple words America needs to heed
With atheist, Unitarianism, Muslim, Hindu, Buddhist
and the list goes on…There is no harmony or rhythm
because of this many find it difficult to sing the same song

One nation under God as it is known or
blessed is the nation whose God is the Lord
If we cannot come together in unity then
how can we go on

I move into the neighborhood and you move out
Separatists, prejudice, and discrimination
the price of tuition and health care are raised
followed by payments to influence legislation
Then without hesitation many of mine experience
higher rates of incarceration

All together now holding hands and pray that God bless
America
Weak and oppressed are preyed upon so are the elderly
and the young…Hello America what page are we on

My country tears of thee, sweet land of liberty
A melting pot we should be, somehow it seems
the greedy comes before the needy

Some sing too fast, too slow, out of tune,
but this is all of our home while some remain silent
choosing not to sing
Are we to gather and make our own interpretation of

what that is suppose to mean...

God bless America

AeA 8/2/07

Freedom*

Some people think they
have to die so that they can be free
While some people are too afraid
to fly, they would rather die

This is a new day for a new way
Breaking from the old
a renewing of the mind, a chance
to put the past behind
With a new chapter that is about to
unfold
Moses is dead and the spirit of Joshua
lives on, a new day has dawned
We did not have to paint the whitehouse
Just changed the occupants and stabilize
the rent
Some folks still scratching their heads
hoping for yesterday, because today
doesn't make much sense

Its been a long time coming
no more fear, no more running
no more tears of sorrow
this is tomorrow

Let us pause for a moment to catch our breath
remembering our forefathers
who can now finally rest

No more chains binding me, now I
just have to set my mind free

Will you lift your voice and cry freedom
Will you lift your mind and declare freedom
Will you embrace your brother and say freedom
Will you respect your sister and say freedom

No more chains binding me,
now I just have to set my mind free

AeA 3/11/09

Chapter Three:
Just Me

We all have personal experiences and thoughts. Often times we do not share them. Perhaps there are some that we should.

Consider this, what you have experienced can be used to improve yourself and/or encourage someone else…Think about it.

Beat Down

Like a one hundred twenty degree day
and there is no shade

Like a sudden hail storm, no place to run
and there is no cover

Like being surrounded by ten angry people
they tell you, that you are in the wrong
neighborhood and here you don't belong

Like a migraine headache that just
will not go away

Thats what it feels like…

Like getting fired from your job, then you
return home and your house has been robbed

Like when you left me…

No note, rhyme, reason, or goodbye
Just a straight up beat down.

AeA 6/15/08

Letting Go*

Several years have passed and your health
has been in decline
life does not come with rewind
Still I loved you, you were mine
As you lie there in your hospital bed
memories and emotions filled my heart and head

Nothing else to save you could be done
there was nothing else they would do
Even at that moment, I could not imagine
my life without you
Thoughts began to form, were you proud of your son

Childhood memories of you and I began to run around
like you teaching me karate and knocking me down
Forgetting all the times you were not there
Even the hurt, anger, and feelings of despair
At this point, I did not care
Our relationship was still special
To put it plainly, I love you so
I just did not want to let you go

Fighting tears I began to pray. As I prayed, you struggled
for every breath. The inevitable was next
I had already begun to miss you. I asked the Lord
for your peace and rest
I kissed you on your head to say goodbye
Never once did I ask the Lord why

His will was done and it had to be so
I asked for strength, it was time for letting go.

In memory of Alphonso Turner

AeA 3/29/08

Who Will Cry

An old man once told me, son you
live fast you die twice, specially when
you go against God's word.

Thought to myself, I don't hear you man
you just old and bitter. This is my life
and its my time. Check out my ice, so
save your words and yo advice

Needless to say, I did not heed
now I am no longer here…Who will cry for me

She says this child is mine. This other female said
this one and that one looks like me. Now I know fo
sho this one is mine. Its by my girl

I do what I can when I can, right now I'm about the
hustle and working it man. Now I'm no longer here.
I spent my time in the street and my child don't
even know me…Who will cry for me

Moms said I could have been anything I wanted.
Gangster, pimp, player, and hustler I chose
I broke her heart and caused her sorrow. Thoughts
of what if and if only still haunt her. For her son
no more tomorrows…Will she cry for me

In the hood with the fellas and rolling with the crew,
crying is something we just don't do. Do you suppose
they might change the rules this one time for me or for you.
In this life I gave it shot. Did my hustle and lost out.
No longer here…Who will cry

AeA 4/4/08

After Thought*

I never wanted this
I had dreams, goals, and plans
Instead I stand before you
with blood stained hands

I never wanted this
I cry inadvertently and
tremor uncontrollably
No one could ever understand
there is no consoling me

I never wanted this
I don't know when I slept last
too many faces, victims, and dark places
too much from my past

I never wanted this
Tell me what is it to smile
or laugh. I can't even imagine
it has been awhile.
I'm at the end, before I could begin

AeA 6/5/08

Conflicted

I hear all the time but do not understand
with all that is going on, for my life
you still have a plan
You say I have a future. For me there
is a purpose and its all in your hands
Meanwhile I'm just trying to understand
this mentality of mine, that continues to
place enmity between you and I

I want you to love me, I want to be free
Sometimes I want help with this something
that seems to be holding, stopping, and
hindering me.
I have tried so many things and so many
ways. Its seems as though I start to go in
circles and lose track of days.

Tripping, stumbling, and constantly falling even
though I ignore your voice inside I know its
you I should be calling

People, family, and friends doing this and saying
that. How do I pull away? I have grown tired
and so weary when I need them most, they
do not see or hear me.
Each time I start to come your way, I see and hear
the church folks talking. Doing what they do
outside while its praise the Lord hallelujah and
being saved and sanctified inside
Most try to keep it low and hide that other side.
Living the life of a lie

The name of God being misused, religion abused
All of this is making me feel confused
I can't keep going through this again and again…

I feel conflicted

AeA 9/25/07

Devil Talk*

You have false idols and Gods
You dance to lyrics that you don't
understand, but make your head bob

You sell, slang, and push dope
to any and all of your own, constantly
robbing them of hope

You break in homes and houses
of one another, then curse the
folks who attempt to assemble you as brothers

You kill one another with total disregard
Then you sit around complaining
that life is so hard

I got you, right where I want you
No one works for me the way that you do
Making heroes out the likes of scarface
as your level of intelligence
is slowly and systematically erased

Their education level continues to soar higher
while lust and greed becomes your only desire

Congratulations, keep slanging and banging
No need to wonder or guess
where in eternity you'll be hanging

I know you don't believe me
but look at your situation
how you are filled with such hate and frustration

You ain't gone do nothing about it
because you are filled with uncertainty,
hesitation, and animosity

Hey, don't blame me
take a look at yourself

I got you in a box
but you don't realize that you hold the key
I'm just glad your ignorance keeps it locked
Your unbelief, envy, and jealously I feed daily
so your loathing becomes solely dependent upon me

Keep doing what you are doing
While everything around you becomes undone
Like a hamster you'll just get back
on the wheel and continue to run

              AeA 7/25/08

Somebody*

I may have gone through
so I can get through just
to be able to arrive at

Sometimes things are worth repeating
a second time in relating will
help with conveying with an alternate
way of stating

What you observed as path
and life of self destruction allowed
God to begin construction which
led to my resurrection

When I was cast down and
appeared broken, talked about
and suffered persecution not realizing
who I was, not listening to
whom I belong…I was still somebody

In spite of myself God had
to show me that I am a vessel
and this vessel is a temple
and this temple is his handy work
apart of his body. A price paid by
his blood and many stripes

A dastardly ploy of deception by the enemy
almost triumphed. I was filled so much
emptiness I believed I was nobody

I always looked at where I was from
and where I was at which prevented me
from seeing or comprehending destiny

My circumstances, environment, and
situation I once allowed to shape and
mold my mind, soul, and body
Until I became a nobody
Value was not there, hope did not exist
At that time love was not on my list
Unknowingly I was still somebody

You are what you eat, as a man think
so is he. What I had to do was
decide will I be just anybody, nobody,
or be who God has created me to be

Somebody

                                                              AeA 2/3/09

Chapter Four:
Between God and I

Allow me to make one thing clear, you do not have to be a believer to read this book or particular chapter. However I encourage you to read this chapter with an open mind.

Personally, I thought I could do or make happen what I wanted too. My destiny, fate, etc. Then Truth came in, an awakening if you will. God is in control and it is better to learn about him and his will. Then you will find your place. (we all have one)

These ten poems that I offer, I am confident will bless you. Read on…Do not be afraid.

By the River*

As the ships go by I pray
As people walk by I pray
When I am alone I praise
by the river

As the currents flow I pray
As the birds sing there song I pray
When I am all alone I praise
by the river

But its time for me to cross over

In preparation I prayed
that you are still moving across the waters
I praised you because I do not
want to be swept under

You have given me so much insight
so many answers
I had my best laughs and cried my
most sorrowful tears…by the river

Stretch your hands toward me and
bid me to come

Its time for me to crossover

As planes fly overhead I pray
As the fish swim by I pray
As the trees sway I pray
When I am alone I praise

by the river

But its time for me to cross over

AeA 3/14/09

A day in the life

At a young age it was foretold by prophecy
that I would preach, a little boy with only
sports on his mind to become a preacher

Though presently being molested unknowingly
being tested, looking back he now sees
the experience as a teacher

The anointing is there even though he doesn't
understand how it is, his mother is receiving
fists and backhands

He often cries when no one is around just
wanting to fly away
Somehow he just cannot seem to leave the ground
yet believing tomorrow will be a better day
Maybe open doors to a better way

Tomorrow comes and its more the same
Family, from which you gather strength
have treated far worse than any enemy
What remains are the thoughts of
the many transgressions and pain
The lies, envy, games, and jealousy
so the boy ponders within himself,
do they really love me

Have I not given them money, prayers, favors,
and my hand
If someone could explain this treatment
because I just don't understand

I have offered more than the other cheek
and given you my hand
You bit it once, twice, more than
seventy times seven
Somehow the boy still looks toward heaven

After failed relationships, marriages, and
encounters with bouts of depression
his head is hung so low
Spiritually depleted, mentally fatigued bordering
on defeat with really no place to go
Is this the perfect situation, crisis, or opportunity to
again invite Jesus in to restore and heal me
Is this time that answers can be found
to reveal ones purpose and destiny
Somehow I feel there has to be more
searching for a reason perhaps just out of
desperation to get up off the floor

Well Jesus here I am
a typical day in my life
If you want me, here am I
Open…Please take my hand

AeA

Why

I ask myself and I have asked the Lord…Why?

Why do I constantly strive to abide
correctly and trouble seems to always dog me

Why does it seem every time
I turn my head from the left
to the right and operate that way
I constantly find strife

Why does it seem as I try to reach up
It feels as though someone is holding my feet
and someone else has their feet standing on
my hands
Can you imagine the pain and anguish
How about the thoughts of frustration and
temptation that enter my brain

Why I have cried so many tears
but here we go again, what seems to
be year after year

A smile for show so the outside world can see

As I cry, scream, and crumble on the inside
I'm just asking…Why?

AeA 2/24/05

Confession

I hear a voice, it keeps calling me
I know it is you Lord, you voice is
like no other I have ever heard

I try to ignore you, not because of
disrespect but because of guilt,
embarrassment, and shame

Still….

You keep calling my name
You said hold your head up, as I
held it down
You tell me to come, I'm afraid
so out of fear I run

Why? Why are you calling me?
I have done so much, said so much
wrong

You said, forgive yourself then ask for mine
I replied, it hurts too much. I'm
afraid to let it all go

Now I feel your touch reassuring me
You said, I called you now trust me
Confess and let it go, you will be free
I will give you new life
Because its all in me
Allow me to do what I do, I am knocking

With tears amassed in my eyes…I slowly
cry out, so much better and so much lighter
I begin to feel

Now louder your name I exclaim! In
exhortation I begin to dance out of control
because you God have forgiven me
That was a burden lifted and a great blessing

My confession

                                                          AeA 6/20/08

Untitled XIII*

Sssh…First you had my ear
then I offered my shoulder now I give you my chest
you can trust me, put me to the test

It began when you were young
and the experiences have made you older
You listened to them saying you were the worse
Now hear me when I say you are the best

I see the tears you cry late at night when
you are all alone. I feel the pain you desperately
attempt to hide, so much you have pent up inside
Relax…Yes it has been rough, so much untold
Hold your head up, no more crawling. From now
on we strut, you have a hand to hold

Some folks do understand there are mistakes
and some mess ups. Then there are some that
do not give second chances or breaks

Don't runaway my child this is a brand new day
I just want you to know you have a friend
Lets take one step at a time
now with confidence, we begin

We no longer look back that's old and passed away
There is a new chapter about to unfold
the frown you once wore is no longer
part of your wardrobe

We look forward to fortunes being turned around

Those tears of sorrow are left in yesterday
now tears of joy fill tomorrow
A smile found that was once lost
remembering trust was the only cost

                                                AeA 6/24/08

Untitled XV*

Yes, I have imperfections that are not of God
but because I set my affections
on pleasing God, I have overcome fleshy desires
Drugs and alcohol no longer can hold or control me
Your tongue that belittled constantly
a reminder of my past must now be silenced and cease

I have now learned of grace and mercy
no longer do I drown in sorrow and pity
My head is held high and I press
Yesterday my excuse for laziness was rest
each step I take draws me nearer to him
and away from guilt and shame
Oh! How I love to exalt his holy name

A clean heart, a renewed spirit, one
day soon I pray that my former oppressors
will prepare to hear and receive it

I absolutely love this life I am living
whatever it is I smile
As I continue to concentrate on sowing
seeds of love and giving
The more we imitate him, the more we
become like him
perfect practice to overcome
imperfections and past transgressions

AeA 8/17/08

Countless Blessings*

Every breath that I breathe
All the thirst and hunger pains
that were quenched and filled
The snares and traps that
were not able to hold me
Every obstacle and obstruction
that was moved and removed
Just the ability to praise your name

Can I begin to count, can I begin to measure
each time my heart ached and became broken
the mending and healing that took place
The attempts on my life through violence
and disease
How many times you have delivered me
Never again your love to be taken for granted
The countless blessings you have rendered
that cannot be measured
I cannot name them all, nor am I worthy
but I can rejoice and thank you for me blessing me

AeA 1/18/09

You Saved Me

On my ship of destiny, sailing into my future
I made preparations for a long time, and now
the time is at hand and its mine

Things happened along the way, storms emerged
I was tossed, driven, and darkness grew
A feeling of doubt began to make me unsure
My shipped wrecked and I began to sink
Never proclaiming to be an expert swimmer
still I stroked hands and feet moving for I knew
I did not want to be lost. I know I could see the
shore in the distance. I was confident I would
not perish but each movement seem to take me
further away from where I knew I belonged

My arms now growing so heavy and weary
Thirst and hunger are my only thoughts as I
grew weaker…Then somehow, someway I started
to become buoyant and renewed. I felt strength
returning to me as I touched land

Dehydrated as I was, tears seemingly endless ran
down my face…You saved me
No one else was around, no one to call upon
In spite of what I attempted and tried on my own
you saw fit to spare my life…You saved me

Funny it seems so many know what is best for them
and the me inside. I now know God is all knowing and
wise. I cry out with thanksgiving so glad to be in the
land of the living, so grateful and definitely more

appreciative than ever before. I do not mind kneeling in front of anyone on any floor. I will never know why you chose to spare my life but each breath I take, each moment I have will be spent being the best I can be. To show my thanks to you for saving me.

AeA 8/10/09

Untitled XX

Do I live til I die
or do I die to live
Shall I possess all
that I can or learn
to give all that I have
Only two roads in life
and they are in opposite directions

Do I take the lead and just go
or do I learn to follow
that I might lead

AeA 1/19/08

I am God*

I transcend time and space
I am the giver of life, peace,
knowledge, even eternity
still you do not know me
constantly you reject me

Alpha and Omega, before the beginning
and after the end
I arranged, planned, and put
everything in its place
However from countless lives daily
I am omitted. Finding fewer are committed

I hear false prophets and arrogant
scientists explain how and when
the world will end
Truth is, they do not even know
when the world began
I hear their educated guesses
called hypotheses
my knowledge they will never grasp
because they have not earnestly sought me to ask

Fanatics kill in my name
reprobate minds take my word
twist, turn, and flip it
They convince you that they are anointed
and become self appointed

I am one that you will
never know or understand

until you submit yourself
and take my hand

Examine my name and study my word
If you hunger and thirst
come before me humbly
wisdom, peace, and joy
will be given to fill thee

I rule with rod and staff, I am full of grace and mercy
I am sovereign…You need to know me
I am God.

                                                              AeA 6/29/08

Bonus Poem:
*A Letter of Communication**

Hello. I am your father, mother, sister, maybe your brother.
I am your neighbor. Maybe I am not sure of our relation
but we need to communicate

It appears to be the norm if we ignore one another,
shout out about one another, do harm to each other, while
the entire time passes without establishing dialogue
with one another

We will withhold thoughts, suggestions, and opinions
from one another. Even hurt, anger, and disgusts for
various reasons but I think the common denominators
are fear, lack of respect, and trust

Miscommunication, false communication, and a lack
of communication is where we are today. Are you
willing to continue on this path that evokes
problems rather than solutions.

I understand this may be a poignant perspective for some,
perhaps the silent thinks that this is long over due
There is time that can be redeemed. However too many
moments can pass which present opportunities that can be
lost forever.

Open, honest, and respectful are very key and vital ingredients
If we desire to build in order that we may grow. Vision and
sight are important too. Do you only focus on what appear to
be abnormalities and differences that has caused you to become
indifferent.

Can you see that there is great need for peace to preserve future generations…You guessed it! Then talk to me. Not at me, nor down to me. We have more in common than you think or have you given that any thought

Books and covers, stereotypes, often lead to bias, prejudice, even hate. Then it is taught hence a circle and vicious cycle. Therefore sight becomes limited and vision like a tunnel. Then you say what it is you think you see and without the entire picture, do you really know me or my story. If you do not talk with me and allow me to share some history the mark will continually be missed and you will have never
known me.

Open, Honest, Respectfully, talk to me.

AeA 5/2/2010

LaVergne, TN USA
22 March 2011

221021LV00001B/124/P